Name
_____

Class
_____

School
_____

MY FIRST 1000 WORD DICTIONARY

Myra Ellis
Illustrated by May Kong

 **FEDERAL PUBLICATIONS**
Singapore • Kuala Lumpur • Hong Kong

© 1987 Federal Publications (S) Pte Ltd
Times Jurong
2 Jurong Port Road
Singapore 2261

First published 1987

ISBN 9971 4 1056 7

Printed in Singapore by Koon Wah Printing Pte. Ltd.

PREFACE

MY FIRST 1000 WORD DICTIONARY has been compiled with the aim of making learning both stimulating and fun for children. This is important for children of elementary school age in whom an eagerness to learn and discover can be so readily instilled.

All the entries are based on wordlists of major textbooks used in the elementary schools. Meanings of all the entries are shown in ordinary sentence form with illustrations in full-color for further clarification.

The entry is printed in bold type. Where there are different meanings for one word, these will be shown in separate sentences. Additional useful information is given alongside certain types of entries:

- the past simple tense and present participle under the verb entries
  e.g. **arrange**   arranged, arranging
- the plurals of noun entries with irregular forms
  e.g. **wolf**   wolves
- the other pronoun forms under the subject pronoun entries
  e.g. **he**   him, his

Certain words have been grouped together under one entry

e.g. **building**	:	school, house, shops, cinema, fire station, factory
machine	:	vacuum cleaner, iron, typewriter, computer, bulldozer, toaster, sewing machine
shape	:	circle, rectangle, square, triangle, cone
tree	:	pine, willow, mango, palm

At the end of the dictionary, there are five supplements covering

- The Calendar
- The Family Tree
- Holidays
- Numbers
- Time

The supplements are designed to enable children to learn a word in the context of the group it is associated with.

The artist has chosen a group of names and given each a special character. They are featured in the illustrations according to the characteristics that suit the mood of a particular sentence. This and the warmth and humor of the illustrations add a unique quality to this dictionary.

I wish all children using this book joy in their discovery!

MYRA ELLIS

Here are the people and animals you will read about in this dictionary. You may want to color them.

Grandfather

Grandmother

Baby

Mr. Smiley

Mrs. Lee

Rita

Frog

Betty

Toby

Mouse

Elephant

Norman

Uncle Bob

Brian

Dick

ndra

Harry

Dog

Father

Mother

Bee

Cat

Witch

Policeman

Postman

Spider

Uncle Bill

Tim

Polly

Jimmy

Sally

Patrick

Monster

act acted, acting

Patrick likes to **act** in the school play.

afternoon

It is after twelve o'clock.
It is **afternoon**.
I have lunch in the **afternoon**.

a an

Sandra has **an** apple and **a** pear.

add added, adding

Uncle Bill is going to **add** one more brick.

again

It rained this morning.
It is raining **again** now.

accident

Polly had an **accident**.
She cut her leg.

afraid

Sally is **afraid** of monsters.

against

The elephant is leaning **against** the wall.

across

The elephant is walking **across** the road.

after

B comes **after** A.

age

Sandra is four years old.
That is her **age**.

1

agree   agreed, agreeing

'Yes, let us race.'
We **agree** to run a race.

all

All these men are digging.

also

Harry wants the book.
Sandra **also** wants the book.

airplane

An **airplane** flies in the sky.
Airplanes carry people and things.

allow   allowed, allowing

I am wearing my father's shirt.
My father **allows** me to wear his shirt.

always

Patrick **always** brushes his teeth in the morning.

alike

These two shapes are **alike**.

These two shapes are not **alike**.

alone

Everyone has left.
Mrs. Lee is **alone**.

am   was

I **am** ten years old.
Last year I **was** nine.

alive

My dog is playing dead but he is **alive**.

along

The cat is walking **along** the wall.

ambulance

An **ambulance** takes people to the hospital.

2

among

Toby is hiding **among** the boxes.
Can you see him?

anchor

An **anchor** stops a boat from moving.
It is very heavy.

and

Jimmy has a bat.
He also has a ball.
Jimmy has a bat **and** a ball.

angry

Uncle Bob is **angry** with Dick.
Dick broke his window.

animals

bat

hippopotamus

guinea pig

mouse deer

Here are some **animals**.

ankle

Brian is holding his **ankle**.

answer
answered, answering

Betty knows the **answer**.
She wants to **answer** the question.

ant

An **ant** is a small insect.
It has six legs.

any

Mrs. Lee does not have **any** food.
Her plate is empty.

anyone

Is **anyone** at home?

anything

Norman does not want **anything** to eat.
He is full.

3

apple

An **apple** is a fruit. **Apples** can be red, green or yellow.

arm

Your hand is at the end of your **arm**. You have two **arms**.

arrive arrived, arriving

The train will **arrive** soon.

aquarium

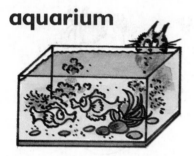

We keep fish in an **aquarium**. It has glass sides.

army armies

An **army** is a large group of soldiers.

arrow

Jimmy shoots his sharp **arrow**.

are were

There **are** two buns on the table. There **were** six buns on the table a minute ago.

around

Grandfather is chasing the monkey **around** the tree.

artist

An **artist** draws or paints.

argue argued, arguing

Sandra and Polly want the bicycle. They **argue** over it.

arrange
arranged, arranging

Mother is **arranging** the flowers in a vase.

ask asked, asking

Harry will **ask** his mother for some dessert.

asleep

The baby's eyes are closed.
He is **asleep**.

attention

Rita is not paying **attention**
to the teacher.

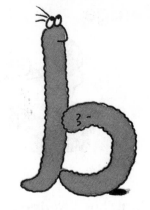

assembly   assemblies

The school children are in
assembly.

aunt

Your **aunt** is the sister of your
father or mother.

baby   babies

This **baby** is drinking some
milk.

astronaut

An **astronaut** travels in a
spaceship.
He can go to the moon.

awake   awoke

The baby's eyes are open.
He is **awake**.

back

Mrs. Lee carries a sack on
her **back**.

at

Brian is waiting **at** the station.
He is looking **at** the train.

away

My friends are leaving.
They are going **away** from
my house.

bad

Norman cannot eat his apple.
It is **bad**.

badge

Harry has a **badge** on his cap.

ball

Dick is kicking a **ball**...
A **ball** is round.

bang banged, banging

A **bang** is a sudden loud noise.
The balloon burst with a big **bang**.

bag

You carry your school books in a **bag**.

balloon

Uncle Bill is blowing up a blue **balloon**.

bank

A **bank** is a safe place to keep money.

bake baked, baking

Grandmother **bakes** food in an oven.

balsam

Balsam is a plant.
It has small flowers.

barbecue

We are having a **barbecue**.
We **barbecue** chicken outside over a fire.

balcony
balconies

This house has a **balcony**.

banana

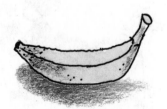

A **banana** is a fruit with a yellow or green skin.

bark barked, barking

A **bark** is the noise a dog makes.
My dog **barks** at cats.

basket

Mother carries her shopping in a **basket**.

bathroom

Toby will take a bath in the **bathroom**.

bean sprout

Sally likes to eat **bean sprouts**. **Bean sprouts** are a vegetable.

bat

We use a **bat** to hit a ball.

beach
beaches

A **beach** is found beside a sea.

bear

A **bear** is an animal with brown or black fur.

bath

Patrick is having a **bath**. He is washing himself.

beak

This bird has an orange **beak**.

beard

This king has a long black **beard**.

bathe   bathed, bathing

We are **bathing** in the sea.

bean

A **bean** is a vegetable. Here are two kinds of **bean**.

beat   beat, beating

The drummer is **beating** his drum.

7

beautiful

These flowers are **beautiful**. They are lovely to look at.

beef

Beef is the meat from a cow.

behind

Harry is walking **behind** his dog.

bed

A **bed** is a place to sleep or rest.
Norman is in his **bed**.

beetle

A **beetle** is an insect.

bell

She rings the **bell**.

bedroom

You sleep in your **bedroom**.

before

You take off your shoes **before** you enter a bathtub.

belong
belonged, belonging

The dog has a bone.
It **belongs** to him.

bee

A **bee** is an insect.
It makes honey.

begin   began, beginning

The play will **begin** soon.
We are waiting for it to start.

below

I can see people **below** me.

belt

Norman wears a black **belt**.

bicycle

A **bicycle** has two wheels.

birthday

It is my **birthday** today. I am five. My brother says, "Happy **Birthday**."

bench   benches

A **bench** is a long seat.

big

An elephant is **big**. A mouse is not **big**.

biscuit

Many children love to eat **biscuits**. These are **biscuits**.

beside

The chair is **beside** the door.

bird

pigeon

woodpecker

sparrow

crow

A **bird** has feathers. Most **birds** fly.

black

This **black** dog is chasing the **black** cat.

between

Harry is sitting **between** his father and his mother.

blackboard

Jimmy writes his name on the **blackboard**.

9

blank

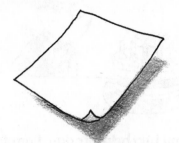

This paper is **blank**.
There is no writing on it.

blouse

Sandra does not like her sister's **blouse**.

body
bodies

You should take care of your **body**.

blanket

A **blanket** is a warm cover.
We put a **blanket** on a bed.

blow   blew, blowing

The wind **blows** the trees.

bone

A dog likes to have a **bone**.
A **bone** is hard.

blind

This woman is **blind**.
She cannot see.

blue

Uncle Bob drives a **blue** car.

book

Mother reads a **book** to me.

blocks

Rita is building a tower with **blocks**.

boat

A **boat** floats on the water.

borrow
borrowed, borrowing

I **borrow** a pen from my sister.
I will return it later.

both

Father will buy bananas and biscuits.
He will buy them **both**.

bow

Mrs. Lee has a **bow** in her hair.

boy

These **boys** are playing soccer.

bottle

He pours a drink from the **bottle**.

bow   bowed, bowing

The man **bows** to the lady.

branch   branches

A **branch** is part of a tree.
Branches grow from the trunk.

bottom

Patrick is at the top of the ladder.
The dog is at the **bottom**.

bowl

Brian has some soup in his **bowl**.

box   boxes

You can keep things in a **box**.
These new shoes are in the **box**.

bread

This shop sells lots of **bread**.
Bread is made from flour.

break   broke, breaking

Glass will **break** if you drop it.

breakfast

We eat **breakfast** in the morning.

bring
brought, bringing

She will **bring** the food to the table.

bubble

A **bubble** is round and filled with air.
It is fun to blow **bubbles**.

breathe
breathed, breathing

We **breathe** in and out all the time.
We **breathe** through our nose.

broom

We sweep the floor with a **broom**.

bucket

The worker carries sand in a **bucket**.

brick

This man is building a wall with **bricks**.

brown

He is wearing a **brown** shirt and **brown** trousers.

buffalo   buffaloes

A **buffalo** is a large, strong animal.

bridge

Uncle Bill is crossing the **bridge**.
The **bridge** is over a river.

brush   brushed, brushing

She scrubs the floor with a **brush**.
Sally **brushes** her hair.

build   built, building

We **build** a house with our blocks.

12

building

Here are some **buildings**.

school

fire station

house

cinema

shop

factory

13

bun

Sandra is eating a **bun**.
It is a sweet cake.

burn　burned, burning

The wood is **burning**.

bus　buses

He wants to catch the **bus**.
A **bus** can carry many people.

bus stop

People get on and off at the
bus stop.

busy

Mrs. Lee has a lot of work to do.
She is **busy**.

but

A giraffe is tall **but** a duck is
short.

butcher

Mother goes to the **butcher** to
buy meat.

butter

We spread **butter** on bread.

butterfly　butterflies

A **butterfly** is an insect.
It has pretty wings.

button　buttoned, buttoning

My shirt has five **buttons**.
I can **button** it myself.

buy　bought, buying

We **buy** things with money.

by

Patrick is standing **by** the bus stop.
He will go to school **by** bus.

calendar

We look at a **calendar** to find the date.

calf   calves

A **calf** is a young cow.

camp   camped, camping

The boys will **camp** here.
There are two tents in this **camp**.
You sleep in a tent when you go **camping**.

cage

These monkeys are in their **cage**.

call   called, calling

Sandra is **calling** to her dog.

can   could

I know how to swim.
I **can** swim.
I **could** not swim last month.

cake

A **cake** is sweet.
It is made from flour, eggs, butter and sugar.

camera

We take photographs with a **camera**.

canary   canaries

A **canary** is a small yellow bird.
It sings sweetly.

15

candle

There is only one **candle** on the cake.

car

Father wants to buy the big **car**.

carpenter

A **carpenter** makes things out of wood.

canna

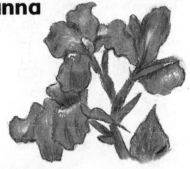

A **canna** is a flower.
Cannas are yellow or red.

card

Sally gave me a **card** on my birthday.
We are playing games with **cards**.

carpet

A **carpet** is used to cover the floor.

canteen

We buy food and drink at the school **canteen**.

careful

I am **careful**.
I will not drop the tray.

carrot

A **carrot** is a vegetable.
It grows underground.

cap

Do you like my new red **cap**?

careless

Dick is **careless**.
He has dropped the plates.

carry   carried, carrying

Sandra can **carry** the puppy home.

16

cart

The ox is pulling the **cart** along the road.

caterpillar

A **caterpillar** has many legs. It will turn into a butterfly.

center

Betty is in the **center** of the circle.

cartoon

Harry likes to watch **cartoons** on television.
Cartoons make him laugh.

cave

A **cave** is a hole in the rock. Bears live in this **cave**.

chair

Is the **chair** too big for Tim?

cat

This **cat** is eating.

ceiling

Father is painting the **ceiling** of the room.

chalk

He likes to draw with **chalk**.

catch　caught, catching

Toby tried to **catch** the ball. Rita **caught** it.

cent

A **cent** is a coin. There are one hundred **cents** in a dollar.

chalkboard

Our teacher writes on the **chalkboard**.

change
changed, changing

The children **change** their clothes after school.

chest

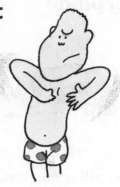

Dick is beating his **chest**.

chocolate

Chocolate is brown and sweet. "Mmm, that **chocolate** looks good."

chase   **chased, chasing**

The policeman **chases** after the thief.

chicken

A **chicken** is a baby hen. **Chickens** are yellow.

choose
chose, choosing

Sally is trying to **choose** a dress.

cheek

Rita is pointing at her **cheeks**.

child   **children**

A **child** is a boy or a girl who is not yet grown up.
These **children** are playing.

chop
chopped, chopping

Mr. Smiley **chops** the wood.

cheese

Cheese is a food made from milk.

chilli   **chillies**

A **chilli** can be red or green. **Chillies** make food taste hot.

chopsticks

The Chinese usually eat with **chopsticks**.

church
churches

Many people go to **church** every Sunday.

city   cities

A **city** is a very large town.

clean

Toby has **clean** hands.
His feet are not **clean**.

cicada

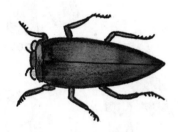

A **cicada** is an insect.
Cicadas make a lot of noise.

clap   clapped, clapping

They **clap** their hands when the play ends.

clear

The water is **clear**.
I can see my feet through it.

circle   circled, circling

11 + 4 = ___   10, 15, 20

Patrick has drawn a **circle** around the answer.
He has **circled** the answer.

class   classes

There are six pupils in this **class**.

clerk

A **clerk** works in an office.
This **clerk** is typing.

circus

A **circus** is a big show.
Polly loves going to the **circus**.

claw

Some birds and animals have **claws** on their feet.

clever

She is **clever**.
Her answers are all correct.

climb
climbed, climbing

Do you like to **climb** trees?

clinic

Norman is ill.
He goes to the **clinic** to see the doctor.

clock

A **clock** tells us what time it is.

close
closed, closing

Mother asked me to **close** the door.

clothes

Clothes are things we wear.

shoes

shirt

shorts

T-shirt

pajamas

socks

tie

trousers

cap

dress

raincoat

skirt

blouse

panties

sandals

stockings

hat

nightgown

cloud

I see a **cloud** in the sky.
Clouds bring rain.

cobra

A **cobra** is a dangerous snake.

coconut

Coconuts grow on trees.
A **coconut** has a hard brown shell.

clown

A **clown** tries to make us laugh.
He wears funny clothes.

cobweb

A spider makes a **cobweb** to catch insects.

coffee

Mrs. Lee drinks **coffee** at breakfast time.

coast

The **coast** is the land by the sea.

cock

A **cock** is a bird.
It does not lay eggs.
It makes a lot of noise when the sun rises.

coin

A **coin** is a piece of money.
Patrick collects **coins**.

cockroach
cockroaches

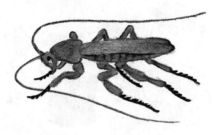

A **cockroach** is a dark brown insect.

cold

The water is too **cold** for Sandra.

collect
collected, collecting

Sally **collects** many sea-shells.
Mother **collects** me from school every day.

come   came, coming

Sandra's mother is telling her to **come** home.

compare
compared, comparing

They **compare** shoes.
His are large but hers are small.

cook   cooked, cooking

Sally is helping her mother to **cook** the dinner.
She wants to be a good **cook**.

corner

There is a tree in the **corner** of the garden.
This table has sharp **corners**.

color
colored, coloring

A rainbow has seven **colors**.
I am **coloring** one in my book.

cone

A **cone** is a shape.
This hat is **cone**-shaped.

correct

Betty has given the **correct** answers.

comb
combed, combing

She is **combing** her hair.
Her **comb** is red.

continue
continued, continuing

Jimmy has stopped playing.
Brian will **continue** for a while.

count   counted, counting

How many flowers are there?
Count them.

22

country   countries

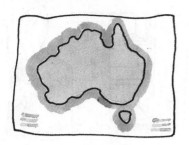

This map shows the **country** of Australia.

crab

A **crab** is an animal with a hard shell.
It has two claws and eight legs.

crawl   crawled, crawling

A baby **crawls** on his hands and knees.

cover   covered, covering

This woman **covers** her child with a blanket.

crane

A **crane** is a machine which lifts things.

crayon

She is drawing with a blue **crayon**.

cow

A **cow** is an animal.
Cows give us milk.

crib

A baby sleeps in a **crib**.

cowboy

A **cowboy** rides a horse and looks after cows and bulls.

crash

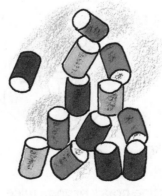

Crash! The tins fell to the floor.

croak   croaked, croaking

After the rain you can hear the frogs **croaking**.

crocodile

A **crocodile** is a large animal that lives in the water.

crowd

A **crowd** is a lot of people all together in one place.

cupboard

Father will mend the **cupboard**.

crooked

This line is **crooked**.
It is not straight.

cry   cried, crying

The baby is **crying** because he is hungry.

curry

Your mouth feels hot when you eat **curry**.

cross   crossed, crossing

They can **cross** the road now.
A **cross** is shaped like + or ×.

cucumber

A **cucumber** is a vegetable.
Cucumbers are green.

cut   cut, cutting

Sally will **cut** the paper with her scissors.

crow

A **crow** is a black bird.
Crows are noisy.

cup

She pours orange juice into her **cup**.

cycle   cycled, cycling

Brian is **cycling** in the park.

24

date

deep

What is the **date** today?
It is the 5th of May.

dance danced, dancing

day

They love to **dance**.
They are **dancing** to the music.

It is **day** when it is light outside.
Do you know the **days** of the week?

The water is **deep**.
It is a long way to the bottom of the pool.

danger

dead

deer

This sign warns you of **danger**.
You must not go in.

The bird is **dead**.
It is not breathing.

A **deer** is an animal.
Deer eat grass and vegetables.

dark

deaf

dentist

It is **dark** at night.

Grandfather is **deaf**.
He cannot hear.

A **dentist** looks after your teeth.

25

desk

We sit at our **desks** to write.

dinner

This **dinner** smells good.
We eat **dinner** in the evening.

divide divided, dividing

Mrs. Lee **divides** the cake.
She will cut it into four pieces.

different

A leopard is **different** from a tiger.
It is not like a tiger.

dirty

Dick is **dirty**. He is not clean.

do did, doing

dig dug, digging

Uncle Bill is **digging** a hole.

dive dived, diving

I **do** my homework when I come home from school.
Mother **does** the cooking.
She **did** the washing this morning.

dining room

A **dining room** is the place in which you eat.

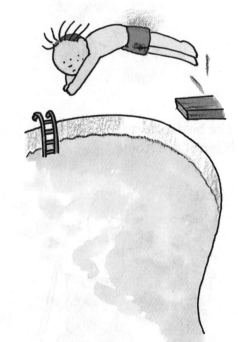

Patrick can **dive** into the swimming pool.

doctor

A **doctor** looks after sick people.

dog

A **dog** is an animal with four legs.
Dogs bark.

door

We go in and out of a house through **doors**.
This **door** is open.

dragonfly dragonflies

A **dragonfly** is an insect. Many **dragonflies** have bright colors on their bodies.

doll

Sandra is playing with her **doll**.

dot

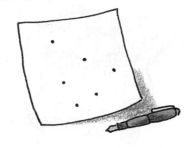

A **dot** is a small mark.
There are **dots** on the paper.

drain

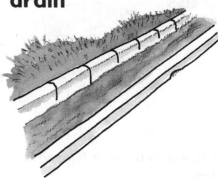

A **drain** carries water away.

dollar

Each week Harry saves one **dollar**.
He now has five **dollars**.

down

Dick goes **down** the slide.

draw drew, drawing

I will **draw** my father.

donkey

A **donkey** is an animal with long ears.

downstairs

Sally is coming **downstairs**.

drawer

Toby keeps his pen in the **drawer**.

27

dream dreamt, dreaming

Sally is asleep.
She is having a **dream**.
She **dreams** she is flying.

drive drove, driving

This man **drives** a bus.

dry dried, drying

The clothes are **dry**.
Mother is collecting them.
We **dry** our hands with a towel.

dress
dresses

Rita wants to wear her red
dress.
She can **dress** herself.

driver

My uncle is a taxi **driver**.
He drives a taxi.

duck

A **duck** is a bird.
Ducks can swim and fly.

drink drank, drinking

You **drink** when you are
thirsty.
Which **drink** would you like?

drop
dropped,
dropping

Mrs. Lee **drops** the vase.

drum

Toby likes to beat his **drum**.

duckling

A **duckling** is a young duck.

dull

This book is not interesting.
It is very **dull**.

28

dump
dumped, dumping

Mother **dumped** the heavy shopping-bag on the table.

early

Uncle Bob is **early**. The shop is not open yet.

during

Norman fell asleep **during** a lesson.

each

Each child wears a different hat.

earth

The **earth** is big and round. It looks like this from the moon. Dogs like to dig in the **earth**.

dust
dusted, dusting

There is a lot of **dust** on this shelf.
Mrs. Lee is **dusting** it.

eagle

An **eagle** is a large bird. It eats small animals and birds.

earthquake

During an **earthquake** the earth moves and cracks.

dwarf

A **dwarf** is a very small person. There are **dwarfs** in some fairy tales.

ear

You hear with your **ears**.

eat
ate, eating

Norman **eats** breakfast at seven o'clock.

egg

Birds lay **eggs**.
Baby birds hatch from **eggs**.

elbow

Your **elbow** is where your arm bends.

electricity

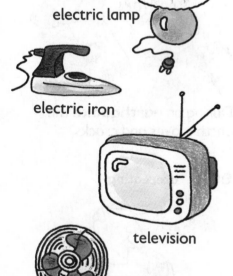

electric lamp

electric iron

television

electric fan

Electricity makes many things work.

elephant

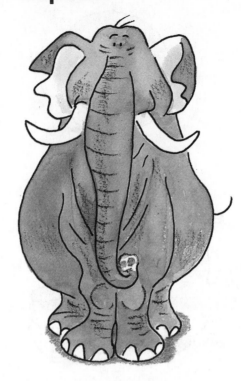

An **elephant** is a large animal.
Elephants have long trunks.

elf   elves

An **elf** is a fairy.
Elves play tricks on people.

empty

His bowl is **empty**.
There is nothing in it.

engine

The car will not go.
Father must repair the **engine**.

enjoy   enjoyed, enjoying

We **enjoy** swimming.
We like it very much.

enough

Tim is tall **enough** to reach the book.
Norman has **enough** to eat.

enter   entered, entering

Our teacher **enters** our classroom.
She is coming in.

entrance

An **entrance** is the way into a place or a building.

envelope

You put a letter in an **envelope**.

escalator

An **escalator** is a moving staircase.

every

There are flowers on **every** table.

exercise
exercised, exercising

They are doing some **exercise**. They are **exercising**.

equal

Brian and Harry have an **equal** number of marbles.

estate

I live on an **estate**. There are many apartments on my **estate**.

exit

An **exit** is the way out of a building.

eraser

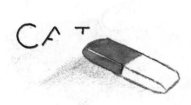

Rita uses an **eraser** to rub out the word.

evening

Evening is the time between day and night.

eye

You see with your **eyes**. Everyone has two **eyes**.

31

fall   fell, falling

Toby is **falling** off his chair.

farm

face

You can see your **face** in the mirror.
Your **face** shows how you feel.

family   families

This is a photograph of Sandra's **family**.

A **farm** is a place for growing food and keeping animals.

factory   factories

A **factory** is a building where things are made.

fan   fanned, fanning

farmer

A **farmer** looks after the plants and animals on his farm.

fairy   fairies

I like to read **fairy** tales.
Fairies can do magic things.

I **fan** myself when I am hot.
A **fan** makes us feel cool.

fast

This car is going very **fast**.

fat

Norman is **fat**.
He eats too much.

fence

Mr. Smiley is putting a **fence** round his garden.

field

A **field** is a large piece of open ground.
There are cows in this **field**.

feather

A **feather** is light and soft.
Birds have **feathers**.

fern

A **fern** is a plant.

fierce

This lion looks very **fierce**.
I will not go near him.

feed   fed, feeding

Sally **feeds** the cat every day.
She gives it milk and fish to eat.

ferry   ferries

A **ferry** is a boat.
This **ferry** is carrying people to the island.

fight   fought, fighting

These dogs are having a **fight**.
They are **fighting** over the bone.

feel   felt, feeling

I **feel** happy when I play with my dog.
My dog's fur **feels** soft.

fill   filled, filling

Harry will **fill** the tank with water.

film

Do you like to watch **films**?
This **film** is about cowboys.

finish   finished, finishing

Tim cannot **finish** the buns.

fireman
firemen

A **fireman** puts out fires.

find   found, finding

Rita cannot **find** her pen.
She is looking for it.

fire

A **fire** is very hot.
We can cook food over a **fire**.

fish

Fish live in water.
Father often goes fishing.

finger

Mrs. Lee has cut her **finger**.

fire engine

A **fire engine** is used to put
out big fires.

fisherman
fishermen

A **fisherman** catches fish.

fingernail

Mother paints her **fingernails**
red.

flag

A **flag** is made of cloth and it
hangs on a pole.

flamingo

A **flamingo** is a bird with long legs.

flat

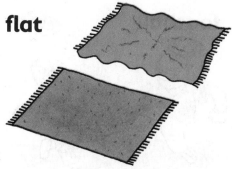

The blue carpet lies **flat** on the floor.
The red one is not **flat**.

flood

In a **flood** water covers the ground.

flower

tulip   daisy

Harry gave his mother some **flowers**.
Many plants have **flowers**.

float   floated, floating

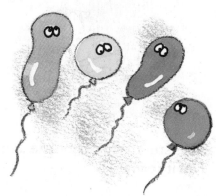

These balloons are **floating** in the air.
Sandra can **float** on top of the water.

floor

The boys are lying on the **floor**.

flour

Mother uses **flour** to make cakes and bread.

fly   flies

A **fly** is a small insect.
Flies have wings.

fly   flew, flying

Birds can **fly**.
They use their wings to move through the air.

35

food

We eat many kinds of **food**.
Here are some of them.

fish

steak

chicken

mango

cabbage

sandwich

cake

peanut butter

cheese

ice-cream

eggs

milk

croissants

jam

butter

bread

foot
feet

Your **foot** is at the end of your leg.
You have two **feet**.

football

They are kicking the **football**.
Football is a good game.

for

My sister cannot open the door.
I do it **for** her.

forehead

She has a mark in the middle of her **forehead**.

forest

There are many trees in a **forest**.

fox
foxes

A **fox** is an animal.
It has a long bushy tail.

fruit

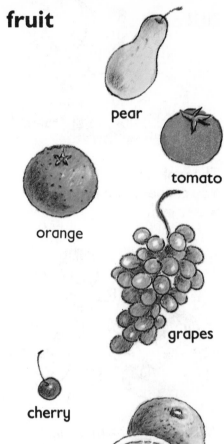

pear

tomato

orange

grapes

cherry

peach

grapefruit

banana

forget   forgot, forgetting

I often **forget** to bring my lunch.
Then I go hungry.

friend

A **friend** is somebody you like very much.

fork

Norman eats his food with a **fork**.

frog

A **frog** is a small animal.
Frogs live in or near the water.

Which **fruit** do you like best?

form   formed, forming

Patrick **forms** a square with the bricks.

front

There is a zipper down the **front** of Dick's shirt.
Polly is standing in **front** of Dick.

fry   fried, frying

Mother is **frying** some chicken.
She is cooking the chicken in hot oil.

full

The tank is **full**.
You cannot put any more
water in it.

fun

We have great **fun** playing in
the water.

funny

He looks so **funny** he makes
me laugh.

fur

Many animals are covered with
soft **fur**

furniture

Here are some pieces of **furniture** we use in the house.

bed

armchair

cupboard

bookcase

dining table

chair

sofa

game

The children are playing a **game**.
What **games** do you like?

hopscotch

basketball

sack race

blindman's buff

card game

skipping

soccer

39

garage

We keep our car in the **garage**.

gate

The **gate** is shut. Jimmy cannot get out.

giraffe

A **giraffe** is a tall animal with a long neck.

garden

A **garden** is a place where flowers or vegetables grow.

ghost

He thought he saw a **ghost**. **Ghost** stories make you feel afraid.

gardener

A **gardener** grows and looks after the plants in a garden.

giant

A **giant** is a very big and tall man.
There are **giants** in some fairy tales.

girl

This **girl** looks beautiful.

gas

My mother has a **gas** cooker.

give   gave, giving

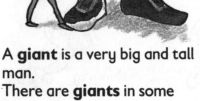

"Please, will you **give** me a sweet?"

glass

Glass is hard and smooth.
Glass will break if you drop it.

go went, going

I **go** to school by bus.

good

This is a **good** book.
I like to read it.

glide glided, gliding

Norman **glides** over the ice.
Dick is **gliding** behind him.

goat

A **goat** is an animal.
Goats can climb well.

goodbye

Sally waves **goodbye** to her friend.

glove

Brian is trying on the **glove**.

gold

Mother would like that **gold** ring.
Gold costs a lot of money.

goose

A **goose** is a large bird with a long neck.

glue

We use **glue** to stick things together.

goldfish

I like to watch my **goldfish** swimming.

grape

A **grape** is a small, round fruit.
Grapes are green, black or red.

grass

Father cuts the **grass**.

green

Green is a color.
Grass is **green.**

ground

He dropped his books on the **ground**.
Plants grow in the **ground**.

grasshopper

A **grasshopper** is a green insect.
Grasshoppers eat plants.

grey

These clouds are **grey**.

groundnut

A **groundnut** grows under the ground.

great

He has climbed up the **great** building.
"**Great**! Now I can see so far," he said.

grocer

A **grocer** sells many things we use in the house every day.
Mrs. Lee is buying milk, sugar and bread from the **grocer**.

group

A **group** of people is waiting for the bus.

greedy

Norman is **greedy**.
He eats too much.

group   grouped, grouping

I will **group** these bricks.
I put the red ones on my left and the blue ones on my right.

42

grow   grew, growing

Harry **grows** taller each year.

h

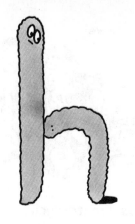

hand

Your **hand** is at the end of your arm.
You hold things with your **hands**.

guinea pig

A **guinea pig** is a small animal. It eats grass.

hair

Hair grows on your head.

handkerchief

Sandra wipes her eyes with a **handkerchief**.

guitar

Toby loves to play the **guitar**.

half
halves

Jimmy cuts his apple in **half**. The two **halves** are of the same size.

handsome

Brian is a **handsome** boy. People like to look at him.

gun

The teacher shoots the **gun** to start the race.

hammer

Uncle Bill is hitting the nail with his **hammer**.

hang   hung, hanging

Rita **hangs** up the clothes.

43

happy

They are **happy** to see their father.

has have

He **has** a motorcycle.
I **have** a bicycle.

he him, his

Jimmy is a boy.
He has a ball.
Rita gave it to **him**.
It is **his** ball.

harbor

There are many ships in the **harbor**.

hat

This **hat** is too big for my head.

head

This is a picture of my **head**.

hard

Stone is **hard**.
It is **hard** to break it.

hatch hatched, hatching

The chickens **hatch** out of the eggs.
They break open their shells.

headmaster

A **headmaster** is the man who looks after a school.

hardworking

Patrick always does his work.
He is **hardworking**.

hawk

A **hawk** is a bird.
It kills other birds and small animals for food.

headmistress

A **headmistress** is the woman who looks after a school.

hear heard, hearing

Can you **hear** the music?
You **hear** with your ears.

height

Father measures my **height**.
I am one meter tall.

help helped, helping

Sally **helps** the old lady cross
the road.

heart

Put your hand on your chest
and you can feel your **heart**
beating.

helicopter

Uncle Bill flies a **helicopter**.

hen

A **hen** lays eggs.

heavy

This stone is very **heavy**.
Tim cannot move it.

hello

Brian said **hello** when he saw
his friend.

here

Please put the flowers **here**.

heel

Your **heel** is the back part of
your foot.

helmet

Mr. Smiley wears a **helmet** on
his head.
The **helmet** keeps his head
from getting hurt.

hibiscus

A **hibiscus** is a flower.
It can be red, yellow, orange
or pink.

hide hid, hiding

The dogs **hide** under the table. Harry cannot see them.

hit hit, hitting

Oh dear! Toby **hit** his head.

home

Your **home** is where you live.

high

This building is very **high**. How **high** can you fly the kite?

hold held, holding

I like to **hold** my doll. I **hold** it in my arms.

hole

Uncle Bob does not see the **hole** in the road.

honey

Bees make **honey**. **Honey** is sweet and good to eat.

hoof hooves

A **hoof** is the hard part of an animal's foot. Cows and goats have **hooves**.

hill

A **hill** is high ground with sloping sides.

holly

At Christmas we decorate our house with **holly**.

hook

Polly hangs her bag on a **hook**.

46

hoop

A **hoop** is a big ring.
The dog jumps through the
hoop.

hospital

You go to the **hospital** when
you are very ill.

house

This is our new **house**.
We are going to live here.

hop   hopped, hopping

Sally can **hop** like a kangaroo.

hot

The sun is shining brightly.
Everyone feels **hot**.

how

I must cross the river.
How can I do it?

horn

Some animals have **horns**.

hotel

A **hotel** is a building where
people away from home can
sleep.

hungry

The children are **hungry**.
They want something to eat.

horse

She rides her **horse** every day.
Some **horses** work for us.

hour

There are sixty minutes in one
hour.
A day has 24 **hours**.

hurt   hurt, hurting

Rita has **hurt** her arm.
It is sore.

ice cube

Jimmy puts an **ice cube** into his drink.
The **ice cube** makes his drink cold.

insect

Insects are small animals with six legs.

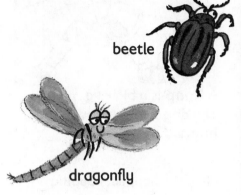

beetle

dragonfly

I   me, my

I am Sandra.
That is **my** book.
Please give it to **me**.

idea

Sally thinks of an **idea** for her story.
She knows what to write.

flea

bee

grasshopper

ice

Ice is very cold.
Ice is frozen water.

ill

Norman is **ill**.
He is in bed.

ladybug

mosquito

ice cream

Norman loves to eat **ice cream**.

in

The apple is **in** the basket.

inside

The lion is **inside** his cage.

into

Mrs. Lee is coming **into** the room.

is   was

This **is** my dog.
I bought him when he **was** a puppy.

jam

Norman puts **jam** on his bread. **Jam** is made from fruit and sugar.

invite   invited, inviting

I **invite** my friend to my party.
I ask her to come to my party.

it

Grandfather has a bag.
He is holding **it**.

jar

What a big **jar** of biscuits!

iron   ironed, ironing

Mother uses an **iron** to **iron** my dress.

jaw

Your **jaw** is part of your mouth. It moves up and down when you are talking or eating.

island

An **island** is land with water all around it.

jacket

I have a red **jacket**.

jeans

Brian is wearing a pair of blue **jeans**.

49

jeep

A **jeep** can travel over rough ground.

jigsaw

Do you enjoy doing **jigsaw** puzzles?

jug

There is a **jug** of water on the table.

jelly

Mother makes good **jelly** from fruit juice and sugar.

jog jogged, jogging

We **jog** round the field.

juice

Jimmy is squeezing the **juice** out of the lemon.

jellyfish

A **jellyfish** lives in the sea.

join joined, joining

Patrick **joins** the strings together.

jump jumped, jumping

The cat **jumps** over the branch. It made a high **jump**.

jetty

A **jetty** is made of wood or stone.

joke

A **joke** is something funny to make you laugh.
Dick is telling Sally a **joke**.

jungle

There are many trees and animals in the **jungle**.

key

Toby will open the door with the **key**.

king

A **king** is the ruler of a country. He lives in a palace.

kangaroo

A **kangaroo** is a big animal that hops.

kick   kicked, kicking

Dick is going to **kick** the ball.

kiss   kissed, kissing

I **kiss** my mother because I love her.

keep   kept, keeping

Harry wants to **keep** the train. He does not want to give it to his brother.

kid

A **kid** is a young goat.

kitchen

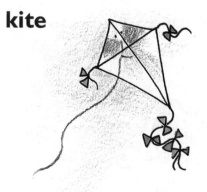

We cook food in the **kitchen**.

kettle

You boil water in a **kettle**.

kind

Sally is a **kind** girl. She gave the hungry boy some food.

kite

My **kite** flies high in the sky.

51

kitten

A **kitten** is a baby cat.

knot

Patrick tied a **knot** in the string.
Can you **knot** your shoe laces?

ladder

Mr. Smiley is climbing up the **ladder**.

knee

Sandra puts her hands on her **knees**.

know   knew, knowing

Betty **knows** the numbers 1 to 10.
She is saying them.

ladle

Polly uses a **ladle** to put soup into her bowl.

knife   knives

A **knife** is for cutting things.
I cut up my food with my **knife**.

lamb

A **lamb** is a young sheep.

knock   knocked, knocking

The postman is **knocking** on the door.

laborer

These **laborers** are helping to build a road.

lamp

A **lamp** gives us light.

land

We stepped off the boat onto dry **land**.

last

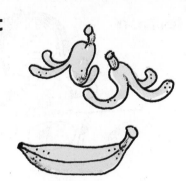

Who will have the **last** banana?

lazy

Norman is **lazy**.
He does not like to work.

lantern

Toby carries a **lantern** to help him see his way.

late

I am **late** for dinner.
Everyone is waiting for me.

lead led, leading

Mother Duck will **lead** her ducklings to the pond.

lap
lapped,
lapping

The cat is thirsty.
He is **lapping** the water.
The baby is sitting on his mother's **lap**.

laugh laughed, laughing

The clown looks funny.
We **laugh** at him.

leaf leaves

A **leaf** grows on a plant.
Most **leaves** are green.

large

Large means big.
The mouse thinks the elephant is **large**.

lay laid, laying

These hens **lay** eggs every day.

learn
learned,
learning

Mrs. Lee is **learning** to ride her bicycle.
Harry showed her how to ride it.

53

leave left, leaving

I will **leave** the house now.
I must go to school.

lemon

A **lemon** is a yellow fruit.
Lemons taste sour.

lesson

We are doing an English
lesson.

left

Patrick is holding up his **left**
hand.

length

Rita measures the **length** of
the table.
She wants to know how long
it is.

letter

I am writing a **letter** to my
grandmother.

leg

ant

bird

rabbit

caterpillar

You use your **legs** to walk.
How many **legs** do these
animals have?

leopard

A **leopard** is a big animal.
A **leopard** has black spots on
its body.

library libraries

You can borrow books from the
library.

less

Sally has **less** cake than Polly.

lick licked, licking

Norman is **licking** his ice
cream.

lift
lifted,
lifting

Patrick is trying to **lift** the basket.

lily lilies

A **lily** is a flower.
Lilies can be orange, white or pink.

list

Father is writing a **list** of chores for me to do.

light

At night we must turn on the **light**.
This feather is **light**.
It is not heavy.

line

I have drawn a **line** down my page.

listen listened, listening

We are **listening** to the story.
We want to hear it.

lightning

Do not play outside when there is **lightning** in the sky.

lion

A **lion** likes to eat meat.
Lions roar.

litter

Put your **litter** into the can.

like
liked,
liking

I **like** to paint.
Brian **likes** to draw.

lips

Mother has red **lips**.

little

Little is small.
This is a **little** baby.

55

live lived, living

Sally **lives** near a school.

long

Polly has very **long** hair.
Dick has short hair.

loud

The airplane is going to fly.
It makes a **loud** noise.

lobster

A **lobster** lives in the sea.
Lobsters have hard shells.

longbean

A **longbean** is a green
vegetable.
Longbeans are thin and long.

love loved, loving

I **love** my father and my mother
very much.
They **love** me too.

lock locked, locking

Toby **locks** the door by turning
the key in the **lock**.

look looked, looking

Look at the monkey.
See how he swings!

low

My chair is too **low**.
I need a higher one.

log

The lumberjacks saw the tree
into **logs**.

lose lost, losing

I often **lose** my pencils.
I cannot find them and I have to
buy new ones.

lunch

You eat **lunch** in the middle of
the day.

machine

A **machine** does work for us.
Here are some.

iron

bulldozer

vacuum cleaner

sewing machine

typewriter

toaster

computer

magic

In my dream I flew on a **magic** carpet.
There is really no **magic** carpet.

magician

A **magician** can do tricks that look like magic.

make   made, making

Mrs. Lee likes to **make** cakes.

man   men

When Harry grows up he will be a **man**.
Harry's father is a **man**.

57

mandarin

A **mandarin** is a small, orange fruit.

marble

We are playing with **marbles**.

market

You can buy many things at a **market**.

mango

A **mango** is a yellow fruit. It has one seed.

march   marched, marching

The soldiers **march** along the road.

many

There are **many** apples on the tree.

margarine

We spread **margarine** on bread.

mask

Patrick has a **mask** on his face.

map

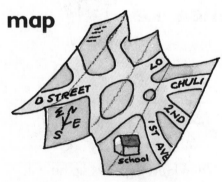

A **map** shows you how to find places.

mark

A **mark** is a spot or stain. Sandra has a **mark** on her cheek.

mat

You wipe your shoes on the **mat**.

match matches

Grandfather uses a **match** to light the fire.
I love to watch a soccer **match**.
Sally's socks **match** but Toby's do not **match**.

mattress
mattresses

I have a new **mattress** on my bed.

may

"**May** I have an ice cream?" asks Sandra.
"You **may**," says her mother.
She allows Sandra to have one.

meal

You eat food at a **meal**.

measure
measured, measuring

Uncle Bill will **measure** the piece of wood.
He wants to know its size.

meat

This shop sells **meat**.
Meat is the flesh of an animal.

medicine

The doctor gives Norman some **medicine**.
It will make him feel better.

meet
met, meeting

Mother **met** Mr. Smiley at the supermarket.

mend mended, mending

I must **mend** my toy.
It is broken.

merry-go-round

We love to sit on the **merry-go-round**.
It goes up and down and round and round.

milk

Milk comes from cows.
It is good for your body.

mirror

I can see myself in the **mirror**.

mine

These men are working in a **mine**.
This cat is **mine**.
It belongs to me.

miss   missed, missing

Polly **missed** the bus.
It left without her.
I will **miss** my grandmother.

meter

Mrs. Lee wants one **meter** of cloth.

mix   mixed, mixing

I **mix** yellow and blue to make green.

middle

The baby is sitting in the **middle** of the rug.
The **middle** flower is red.

minute

There are sixty **minutes** in one hour.
One **minute** is sixty seconds long.

money

We use **money** to buy things.

monkey

A **monkey** has a long tail.
Monkeys like to swing in trees.

mop

Grandmother uses a **mop** to clean the floor.

mosquito mosquitoes

A **mosquito** is a small insect.
Mosquitoes bite people.

monster

Jimmy is reading a story about an ugly **monster**.

more

Norman has already eaten his ice cream.
He would like some **more**.

most

Patrick has some sweets.
Sally has more sweets than Patrick.
Norman has the **most** sweets.

month

This **month** is February.
Next **month** will be March.

morning

It is **morning** when the sun rises.
We have breakfast in the **morning**.

mother

I love my **mother**.
She takes good care of our family.

moon

At night you can see the **moon** in the sky.

morning glory

Morning glory is a purple flower.
The plant grows along walls or fences.

motorcycle

Mr. Smiley goes fast on his black **motorcycle**.

61

mountain

A **mountain** is bigger and higher than a hill.

move moved, moving

We will **move** the table.
We will put it by the window.

muscle

Every **muscle** in your body helps you to move.

mouse mice

A **mouse** has a long tail.
These **mice** like cheese.

much

How **much** do the cakes cost?
Does your thumb hurt **much**?

museum

We are visiting the **museum**.
We look at many old things.

mouse deer

A **mouse deer** is a small animal found in Asia and Africa.

mud

Norman has fallen into the **mud**.
Mud is soft, wet earth.

music

They are making **music**.
Music is made up of sounds we like to hear.

mouth

You use your **mouth** to talk and eat.

mug

Grandfather is holding a **mug** of tea.

must

I **must** run or I will get wet.

mutton

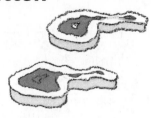

Mutton is the meat from a sheep or a goat.

name

Betty has written her **name** on her book.

near

Jimmy is swimming **near** the edge of the pool.
The edge is not far from him.

my

This is **my** pencil.
I bought it.

narrow

The doorway is too **narrow** for Norman to go through.

neck

Your **neck** joins your head to your body.

naughty

necktie

Uncle Bob is wearing a green **necktie**.

nail

Uncle Bill is hammering a **nail** into the wood.

Dick is very **naughty**.
He is drawing on the wall.

need   needed, needing

Toby **needs** new shoes.
One shoe has a hole in it.

needle

Mother is pulling the thread through the **needle**.

new

I have a **new** bicycle.
I am riding it for the first time.

night

It is dark during the **night**.

neighbor

Your **neighbor** lives in the house next to yours.

news

News is something that has happened.
We watch the **news** on television.

nobody

There is **nobody** in the park.

nest

Birds live in a **nest**.
Nests are made of sticks and leaves.

newspaper

People read the **newspaper** to find out the news.

noise

The children are making a lot of **noise**.
It is very noisy.

never

Never play with matches.
Don't play with them at any time.

next

Rita is standing **next** to Polly.

none

The cat wants some milk.
There is **none** left.

noodles

We are eating **noodles** for lunch.

nurse

A **nurse** looks after sick people.

ocean

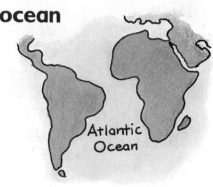

Atlantic Ocean

The **ocean** is a very big sea.

nose

You breathe and smell things with your **nose**.

nut

hazel nut

groundnut

walnut

I like eating **nuts**.
Nuts have shells.

octopus

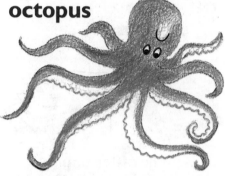

An **octopus** lives in the sea.
It has eight arms.

nothing

There is **nothing** in this box.
It is empty.

of

All **of** us have a cup of milk.
The cups are made **of** plastic.

number

Each player has a **number** on his T-shirt.

oar

You use an **oar** to row a boat.

off

Harry took **off** his muddy shoes and scraped the mud **off** them.

office

These people work in an **office**.

oil

Uncle Bill puts **oil** in the engine.

only

Brian is the **only** boy in the group. The others are all girls.

office boy

Oliver is an **office boy**.
He helps to keep the office tidy and posts the letters.

oil palm

An **oil palm** is a tree.
There is oil in its fruit.

open

The door is **open**.

officer

Uncle Bob is an **officer** in the army.
He tells the soldiers what to do.

old

My trousers are **old**.
I have had them a long time.

opposite

I will sit down **opposite** Sally.
Down is the **opposite** of up.

often

Grandmother **often** comes to visit us.
She comes to see us many times.

on

The food is **on** the table.

or

I can have some chocolates **or** some sweets.
I cannot have both.

orangutan

An **orangutan** has brown hair and long arms.
It lives in the jungle.

orchid

An **orchid** is a flower.
There are many kinds of **orchids**.

oven

Mother puts cakes in the **oven** to cook.

orange

An **orange** is a round fruit.
Orange is a color.

organ

Rita can play the **organ**.
An **organ** makes music.

over

Jimmy jumps **over** the box.

orchard

An **orchard** is a field of fruit trees.
This is an apple **orchard**.

out

We pulled Norman **out** of the hole.

owl

An **owl** is a bird with big eyes.
You can see **owls** at night.

orchestra

An **orchestra** is a group of people who make music together.

outside

Uncle Bill is working **outside** his house.

own

Sandra has her **own** puppy.
It belongs to her.

pain

Norman has a **pain** in his stomach.
It hurts him.

papaya

A **papaya** is a large fruit. Its flesh is red or orange.

pack   packed, packing

We **pack** our bags to go on vacation.

paint   painted, painting

The men are **painting** lines on the road.
They are using yellow **paint**.

paper

We write and draw on **paper**.
Mother wraps the present in colored **paper**.

page

We write and draw on **paper**.

Patrick turns the **page** of his book.

pair

Toby has a new **pair** of shoes.
A **pair** means two things that belong together.

parachute

pail

Toby takes water from the well with a **pail**.

palm

Rita looked at the **palm** of my hand.

A **parachute** helps you fall safely to the ground.

parcel

The postman brought me a **parcel**.

part

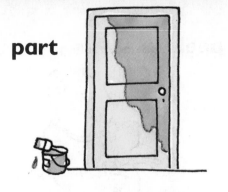

Harry has painted **part** of the door blue.
The other **part** is yellow.

pavement

People walk on the **pavement** by the side of a road.

park   parked, parking

Uncle Bob is trying to **park** his car.
I am playing with my friends in the **park**.

party

We are all enjoying the **party**.

paw

My dog has one white **paw** and three black **paws**.

pat   patted, patting

Mother **pats** the baby to sleep.
She gives the baby a **pat** on the leg.

pay   paid, paying

Polly handed over some money to **pay** for the bread.

parrot

A **parrot** is a bird.
You can teach a **parrot** to talk.

pattern

Mother uses a **pattern** to make her dress.

peacock

A **peacock** is a bird.
Peacocks have beautiful tail feathers.

pear

We are picking **pears** from the trees.
Pears are good to eat.

peel   peeled, peeling

You **peel** the skin off a banana before you eat it.

pencil

A **pencil** is for writing or drawing.

pea

A **pea** is a small round vegetable.
Peas are green.

peep   peeped, peeping

I am **peeping** through a hole in the wall.

penguin

A **penguin** is a bird that lives in very cold places.
Penguins cannot fly.

pedestrian

A **pedestrian** is a person who is walking along the road.

peg

Rita is using **pegs** to hang out the clothes.

people

There are a lot of **people** on the beach.

pedestrian crossing

You cross the road at a **pedestrian crossing**.

pen

I write with my **pen**.
A **pen** uses ink.

person

There is an image here

Jimmy is the only **person** in the classroom.

pet

dog

cat

rabbit

tortoise

goldfish

A **pet** is an animal you like and look after.
These animals are kept as **pets**.

photograph

This is a **photograph** of my grandfather and grandmother.

picnic

We are having a **picnic** in the park.

piano

Sally plays the **piano** very well.
A **piano** makes music.

picture

I am drawing a **picture** of myself.

petal

This flower has five red **petals**.

pick   picked, picking

He is **picking** up the toy.
We must not **pick** the flowers in the park.

piece

Norman is eating a **piece** of cake.

petticoat

Polly has a pretty **petticoat**.

pickle

Uncle Bob likes to eat **pickles** with his sandwiches.

pig

A **pig** is a farm animal.
Pigs are kept for their meat.

piglet

A **piglet** is a young pig.

pineapple

A **pineapple** is a large sweet fruit.
It has yellow flesh.

place

Harry went to these **places** today.

zoo

pillow

Toby is sleeping on two **pillows**.

pink

Sandra has a new **pink** dress.

beach

pilot

A **pilot** flies an airplane.

pipe

The **pipe** has a hole in it.

pin

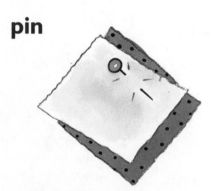

The **pin** is holding the cloth together.

pirate

A **pirate** robs ships at sea.

playground

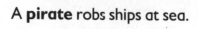

plant
planted, planting

Father will **plant** the flowers. He has many **plants** in the garden.

play
played, playing

After school we **play** a game of marbles.

pocket

I keep my handkerchief in my **pocket**.

plastic

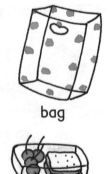

pail

bag

lunch box

raincoat

These things are made of **plastic**.
Some **plastic** is soft and some is hard.

playground

There are swings and see-saws in this **playground**.

point
pointed, pointing

Patrick is **pointing** to the tree.
My pencil has a sharp **point**.

please

When you want something, say **please**.

pole

plate

We put food on a **plate**.

plenty

Mrs. Lee has **plenty** of food. She does not need any more.

Toby is trying to climb the **pole**.

police station

Rita has lost her bag.
She goes to the **police station** to ask the police to help her find it.

policeman
policemen

The **policeman** is stopping the traffic.

pond

We can see many fish in the **pond**.

pony

A **pony** is a small horse.

pool

We love to splash in the **pool**. The rain makes **pools** of water in my garden.

poor

This man is **poor**.
He does not have much money.

pork

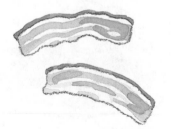

Pork is the meat from a pig.

port

A **port** is a safe place for ships to stay.

post   posted, posting

Patrick buys stamps at the **post** office.
He **posts** a letter and a parcel there.

postman
postmen

The **postman** brings letters to your home.

74

pot

The food is cooking in the **pot**.

pray
prayed,
praying

These people are **praying**.
People **pray** in different ways.

pretty

These flowers are **pretty**.
They are nice to look at.

potato   potatoes

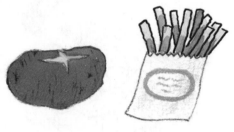

A **potato** is a vegetable.
There are many different ways
to cook **potatoes**.

praying mantis

A **praying mantis** is a green
insect.

prince

A **prince** is the son of a king
and a queen.

pour   poured, pouring

He is **pouring** water into a
glass.

present

There are many **presents** for
Polly on her birthday.

princess
princesses

A **princess** is the daughter of a
king and a queen.

prawn

A **prawn** lives in the sea.
Prawns are good to eat.

press
pressed,
pressing

Sandra is trying to **press** the
door-bell.

prize

Toby won first **prize**.
He ran well.

pull   pulled, pulling

My dog tries to **pull** me along.

puppy

A **puppy** is a young dog.

push   pushed, pushing

I **push** my bicycle up the hill.

punch   punched, punching

It is not kind to **punch** anybody.

purple

We are painting this wall **purple**.

put   put, putting

Mother **puts** the baby into the crib.

pupil

We are painting this wall

The teacher is talking to his **pupils**.

puzzle

Betty does not know which piece to put in the **puzzle**.

puppet

It is fun to play with **puppets**.

purse

Mrs. Lee has too much money in her **purse**.

python

A **python** is a large snake.

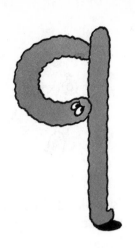

queen

A **queen** is a king's wife.
Some **queens** rule a country.

quite

It is **quite** dark.
It will be darker soon.

quack
quacked, quacking

Ducks **quack**.
A **quack** is the noise made by a duck.

question

He asks her a **question**.

quarrel
quarreled, quarreling

They are **quarreling**.
They are angry with each other.

quick

We must be **quick** or we will get wet.

rabbit

A **rabbit** is a small animal.
It has long ears.

quarter

I have painted in a **quarter** of the square.

quiet

You must be **quiet** in the library.
You must not make a noise.

race

Jimmy is racing with Toby.
Who is going to win the **race**?

radio

Brian is listening to the **radio**.
We can listen to news and
music on the **radio**.

rainbow

Look at the **rainbow** in the
sky.
It has seven colors in it.

rattle

The baby is shaking the **rattle**.
It makes a noise.

railway

A train moves on the **railway**.
People get on and off the trains
at the **railway** station.

raincoat

A **raincoat** keeps you dry
when it is raining.

rash

Norman has a **rash** all over his
body.

raw

All this food is **raw**.
It has not been cooked.

reach
**reached,
reaching**

The dog cannot **reach** the
meat.
It is too short.

rain

Rain is water that falls from
the sky.

rat

A **rat** is an animal.
Rats have long tails.

read   read, reading

Mother **reads** me a story
before I go to sleep.

ready

We are **ready** to go swimming.
Rita is not **ready**.
She still has her clothes on.

rectangle

A **rectangle** is a shape with four sides.

repair   repaired, repairing

Uncle Bill must **repair** his truck.
It will not start.

real

Toby has a **real** dog.
Polly's dog is not **real**.

red

Polly has a **red** ball.

reply   replied, replying

Patrick will **reply** to his friend's letter.
He will write back.

recess

It is time for **recess**.
We will have a short break from our lessons.

refrigerator

A **refrigerator** keeps food and drinks cold.

rest

Toby takes some of the chocolate.
He gives his friend the **rest**.
Grandmother takes a **rest** when she feels tired.

record

Sally will play her new **record**.
It has children's songs on it.

remember
remembered, remembering

Jimmy cannot **remember** which way to go.

restaurant

We like to eat in this **restaurant**.

rich

The king has a lot of money.
He is **rich**.

ring rang, ringing

I will **ring** the bell.
The telephone is **ringing**.

rhinoceros

A **rhinoceros** is a large animal
with a thick skin.
It has one or two horns on
its head.

ride rode, riding

Sally is learning to **ride** a horse.

river

He is rowing down the **river**.

ribbon

Polly will tie a pink **ribbon**
around the present.

right

2 + 4 = 6

Betty gave the **right** answer.
The car is turning **right**.

road

There are many cars on the
road.

rice

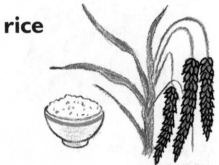

Rice is food.
Rice can be cooked in many
ways.

roar
roared,
roaring

Can you hear the lion **roar**?

80

rock rocked, rocking

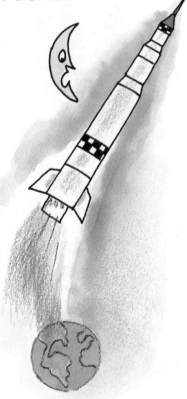

We love to climb over the **rocks**.
Grandmother is sitting in a **rocking** chair.

rocket

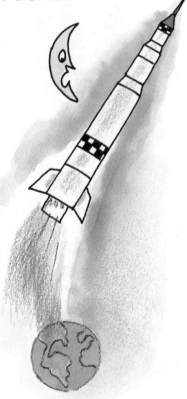

A **rocket** travels into space.

roll rolled, rolling

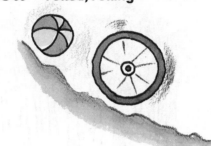

A ball and a wheel are **rolling** down the hill.

roof

Our house has a red **roof**.

room

Harry cannot get inside the **room**.
There are many people inside the **room**.

root

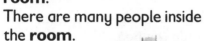

Every plant has **roots** which grow under the ground.
They take in water for the plant.

rope

They pulled Toby up with a **rope**.

rose

A **rose** is a flower.
There are **roses** of different colors.

rough

It is difficult to ride on a **rough** road.

round

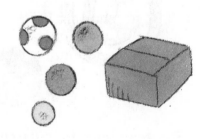

These balls are **round**.
The box is not **round**.

row
rowed, rowing

Toby arranges the chairs in a **row**.
They are in a straight line.
Jimmy is **rowing** across the lake.

rubber

eraser

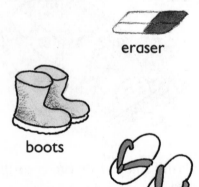
boots

slippers

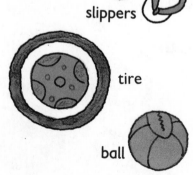
tire

ball

Rubber comes from a tree.
These things are made from **rubber**.

rubber estate

Many rubber trees grow on a **rubber estate**.

rubber tapper

A **rubber tapper** taps trees with a knife.
This lets the juice out of the trunk.

rug

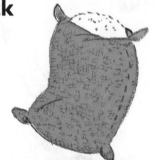

There is a **rug** on the floor beside the bed.

ruler

A **ruler** helps you to draw straight lines.
It helps you to measure things.

run
ran, running

Can you **run** as fast as I can?

sack

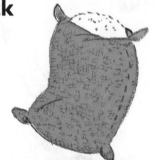

A **sack** is a big bag.
Here is a **sack** of rice.

sad

Sally has lost her pen.
She feels **sad**.

safe

The three kids are **safe**.
The wolf cannot reach them.

same

We each have the **same** book.

saucepan

You cook food in a **saucepan**.

sail   sailed, sailing

My boat has a yellow **sail**.
We are **sailing** to the other
side of the lake.

sand

Beaches are full of **sand**.
Brian is drawing in the **sand**.

saucer

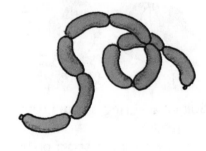

Mrs. Lee puts her cup on the
saucer.

sandals

Sandals are cool to wear in
hot weather.

sausage

A **sausage** is made of meat.

salt

Sally puts **salt** on her food.
She likes salty food.

sandwich
sandwiches

A **sandwich** is two slices of
bread with a filling in between.

saw
sawed, sawing

Uncle Bill cuts the wood with
his **saw**.
He will **saw** it in half.

say said, saying

"Good morning, Mother," **say** the children.

scissors

Polly is cutting the paper with a pair of **scissors**.

sea

The **sea** is the salty water all around the coast.
Many fish live in the **sea**.

scare scared, scaring

Harry is trying to **scare** his sister.
He wants to frighten her.

scream
screamed, screaming

Sandra **screams** when she sees a mouse.
She is scared of mice.

seagull

A **seagull** is a bird which lives near the sea.

scarf

Sally is wearing a **scarf** round her neck.
Rita is wearing a **scarf** on her head.

screw screwed, screwing

A **screw** holds things together.
Mr. Smiley will **screw** the leg to the chair.

seat

stool

chair

A **seat** is something for us to sit on.

school

We go to **school** to learn and play.

screwdriver

He is using a **screwdriver** to put in the screw.

second

A **second** is a very short time.
There are sixty **seconds** in one minute.

84

secret

Rita tells Polly a **secret**. Nobody else can hear what she is saying.

see   saw, seeing

Sandra can **see** three snails. Can you **see** them?

seed

This **seed** will grow into a plant.
You can find **seeds** in many fruits.

see-saw

They are playing on the **see-saw**.
It goes up and down.

sell   sold, selling

These men **sell** drinks.

set

Brian bought this **set** of color pencils.
Uncle Bill bought a **set** of tools.

sew
sewed, sewing

Grandmother is **sewing** the button onto the shirt.

shade

The dog is sitting in the **shade** of the tree.
It is cool in the **shade**.

shadow

My **shadow** is long.
The pole's **shadow** is even longer.

shake   shook, shaking

Jimmy and Patrick are **shaking** hands.

shallow

The water is too **shallow**.
I cannot swim in it.

shape

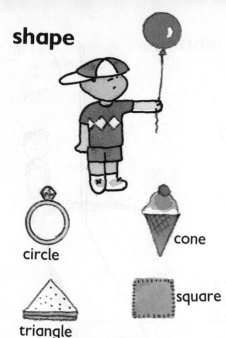

circle

cone

triangle

square

rectangle

The **shape** of a balloon is round.
These things have different **shapes**.

sharp

This knife is very **sharp**.
It cuts the meat easily.

sharpener

Jimmy is using a **sharpener** to make his pencil sharp.

shell

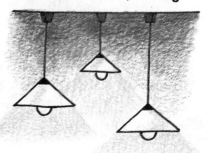

I found a **shell** on the beach.
Eggs and nuts have **shells**.

shine shone, shining

The lights **shine** in the dark.

share shared, sharing

Sally **shares** her sweets with her friends.
She gives her friends some of her sweets.

she her, hers

Sandra is a girl.
She has a doll.
Mother gave it to **her**.
It is **hers**.

ship

A **ship** carries people and things across the sea.

shark

A **shark** is a large fish.
Sharks live in the sea.

sheep

A **sheep** is a farm animal.
It is covered with wool.

shirt

Do you like my new **shirt**?

shoe

Sandra has put on one **shoe**.

short

Tim's trousers are too **short**.

shut   shut, shutting

The door is **shut**. It is not open.

shoot   shot, shooting

He wants to **shoot** the duck with the gun.

shorts

Brian is wearing red **shorts**.

sick

Norman is **sick**.
He does not feel well.

shop

A **shop** sells things.
This **shop** sells toys.

shovel

Uncle Bill uses a **shovel** to dig a hole.

side

Father is washing the **side** of the car.

shopkeeper

A **shopkeeper** sells things.
This **shopkeeper** sells shoes.

show   showed, showing

Harry is **showing** a frog to his sister.
We watched a **show** on television.

signal

The **signal** is green.
The train can go.

sing   sang, singing

Patrick likes to **sing** in the bath.

size

Norman needs larger **size** shoes.
These are the wrong **size**.

skirt

I am wearing a blue **skirt**.

sink   sank, sinking

The marbles **sink** to the bottom of the water.
Sally washes the plates in the **sink**.

skate
skated,
skating

Dick is learning how to **skate**.
These are ice **skates** and roller **skates**.

sky   skies

I can see an airplane in the **sky**.

sit   sat, sitting

Grandfather **sits** on the bench.

skin

Skin covers the whole of your body.

sleep   slept, sleeping

You **sleep** in your bed.
You feel fresh after a good night's **sleep**.

sitting room

We watch television in our **sitting room**.

skip   skipped, skipping

Polly can **skip** with her rope.

slice

Sandra takes a **slice** of bread.

slide   slid, sliding

Dick likes to play on the **slide**.
You may **slide** on a slippery
ground.

slip   slipped, slipping

It is easy to **slip** on a wet floor.

slippery

Wet soap is **slippery**.

slow

My sister is **slow**.
We have to wait for her.

small

This shirt is too **small** for
Norman.

smell   smelled, smelling

I can **smell** the cakes.
They have a lovely **smell**.

smile   smiled, smiling

He asked them all to **smile**.
Each person has a **smile** on his
face.

smoke   smoked, smoking

There is **smoke** coming from
the fire.
Uncle Bob is **smoking** a pipe.

smooth

A sheet of glass is **smooth**.

snail

A **snail** moves very slowly.
It has a shell on its back.

snake

A **snake** slides along the
ground.

89

snow snowed, snowing

Snow falls when it is very cold.
It is **snowing** outside now.

soft

The fur of a rabbit feels **soft**.
Voices and music can be **soft** too.

song

We sing a **song** at Polly's party.

soldier

He is a **soldier** in the army.
An army has many **soldiers**.

sore

My thumb feels **sore**.
I cut it when I fell.

soap

Mrs. Lee washes her hands with **soap**.

some

Norman has **some** bread and some biscuits.
He wants **some** milk too.

sorry

Dick broke Uncle Bob's window.
He is **sorry**.

sock

There is a hole in one of my **socks**.

sometimes

Mother **sometimes** gives me sweets.
She does not give me sweets all the time.

sound

Grandmother hears a loud **sound**.
A **sound** is any kind of noise.

soup

Soup is made from meat or vegetables.
I like to eat bread with my **soup**.

spade

Toby is digging with a **spade**.

splash   splashed, splashing

It is fun to **splash** in the water.
Sally is making a big **splash.**

sour

A lemon tastes very **sour**.
It is not sweet.

speak   spoke, speaking

Do not **speak**.
Grandfather is asleep.

spoon

I am eating with a **spoon**.

space

Stars are in **space**.
There is **space** for another person on this bench.

spider

A **spider** is a small animal with eight legs.
Spiders catch insects in their webs.

spots

This dog has black **spots** all over its body.

spaceship

A **spaceship** travels through space.

spinach

Spinach is a vegetable.
Spinach has green leaves.

square

A **square** has four sides.
All the sides are of the same length.

squeeze
squeezed, squeezing

I **squeeze** toothpaste onto my toothbrush.

stairs

Sally and Patrick climb the **stairs** to reach the top.

stars

The sky is full of **stars** tonight.

squirrel

A **squirrel** has a bushy tail.
Squirrels love to eat nuts.

stamp
stamped, stamping

start   started, starting

We are ready to **start** the race.

stadium

We are **stamping** our feet.
What a noise!
We use **stamps** to send letters and cards in the post.

stay   stayed, staying

Sandra will **stay** at home.
Her brother is going out.

There are many people in the **stadium**.
They have come to watch a soccer match.

stand   stood, standing

The baby can **stand** up by himself now.

steal   stole, stealing

The thief **steals** Mrs. Lee's bag.
He takes something that does not belong to him.

steel

scissors

spoon

knife fork pan

Steel is a hard metal.
All these things are made of
steel.

stick   stuck, sticking

I have a **stick** to put on the fire.
Polly will **stick** the picture into
her book.

stomachache

Norman has a **stomachache**.
His stomach is sore.

stem

The **stem** of the plant has
grown out of the ground.
It has leaves and flowers on it.

stone

A **stone** is a piece of rock.
I found this **stone** on the
beach.

step   stepped, stepping

Harry takes a large **step** over
the water.
His dog has **stepped** into it.

still

Stand **still**.
Do not move.

stomach

The food you eat goes into
your **stomach**.

stop   stopped, stopping

The light is red.
Mother **stops** the car.

storm

During a **storm** the sky is dark
and the wind blows hard.
It rains and there may be
thunder and lightning.

storeroom

Mrs. Lee keeps many things in her **storeroom**.

straw

Jimmy likes to drink through a **straw**.

stripe

A **stripe** is a long narrow mark. These things and animals have **stripes**.

story   stories

Grandfather is telling us a **story**.
He knows many good **stories**.

strawberry
strawberries

A **strawberry** is a small red fruit.

stove

Mother cooks food on a **stove**.

street

A **street** is a road in town with houses along it.

strong

Father is **strong**.
He can carry the heavy box.

straight

I can draw a **straight** line.
Sally's line is not **straight**.

string

I tie up the parcel with **string**.

submarine

A **submarine** is a ship that travels under water.

subtract
**subtracted,
subtracting**

If I take away two apples, I have one left.
I have **subtracted** two apples.

sunburn

Toby has **sunburn**.
He was in the sun for too long.

supper

Before Sandra goes to bed she eats **supper**.

suck   **sucked, sucking**

A baby likes to **suck** his thumb.
Do you like to **suck** sweets?

sunflower

A **sunflower** is a large yellow flower.
It is a tall plant.

surprise

We have a nice **surprise** for mother.
We are giving her some flowers.

sugar

Sugar makes food and drink taste sweet.

supermarket

swallow

A **swallow** is a small bird.
It has long wings and eats insects.

sun

The **sun** gives us light during the day.

We can buy all kinds of food in the **supermarket**.

swan

A **swan** is a white or black bird with a long neck.

sweep

Rita must **sweep** the floor.
It is dirty.

swimming pool

The children swim in the
swimming pool.

sweets

Sweets are made from sugar.
You should not eat too many
sweets.

swing
swung,
swinging

Sally is **swinging** high on the
swing.

T-shirt

I do not know which **T-shirt** to
buy.

sweet potato
sweet potatoes

Sweet potato is a vegetable.
Sweet potatoes grow under
the ground.

sword

Toby and I each have a **sword**.

table

A **table** is a place for eating,
writing, playing a game and
other things.

swim   swam, swimming

I move my legs and arms in the
water when I **swim**.

syrup

Syrup is made from sugar and
water.
It is sweet and thick.

tadpole

A **tadpole** grows into a frog.

tail

The monkey is hanging by its **tail**.

tame

These animals are **tame**. They are not wild.

taxi

A **taxi** is a car. We have to pay to ride in a **taxi**.

take   took, taking

Sandra **takes** the letter to her mother.

tank

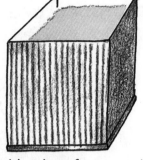

A **tank** holds a lot of water, oil or gasoline. This is a water **tank**.

tea

My parents drink **tea** in the afternoon.

talk   talked, talking

Mother likes to **talk** with her friend.

tap

Toby is turning on the **tap**.

teach   taught, teaching

Uncle Bill is showing me how to swim. He is **teaching** me.

tall

Tim is **tall**. Harry is not **tall**.

taste
tasted, tasting

I do not like the **taste** of lemons. They **taste** sour.

teacher

Our **teacher** will teach us numbers today.

tear
tore, tearing

Sally is crying.
A **tear** is rolling down her face.
I will **tear** the paper before I
throw it away.

tell
told, telling

"Can you **tell** me the way to
the railway station?"

temperature

My whole body feels hot.
I have a **temperature**.

term

Our school **term** starts today.
Our vacation has ended.

thank
thanked, thanking

"**Thank** you for the present,"
said Sandra to her brother.

telephone

Patrick talks to his friend on the
telephone.

temple

Mrs. Lee is praying in the
temple.

that
those

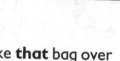

I would like **that** bag over
there.
Those are all too big.

television

Uncle Bob is repairing the
television set.
TV is short for **television**.

tent

It is fun to sleep in a **tent**.

the

Toby is climbing a tree.
The tree is tall.

theater

We are watching a play at the **theater**.

they   them, their

They are doing **their** sewing. The teacher showed **them** how to sew.

think   thought, thinking

Patrick will **think** about a present for his mother. What can he buy for her?

their

That house belongs to the Thompsons. It is **their** house.

thick

The red book is **thick**. It has many pages.

thirsty

When I am **thirsty** I have a drink.

there

The bicycle over **there** is mine.

thief   thieves

A **thief** has stolen our television set.

this   these

This boy is my son. **These** boys are playing.

thermometer

Mother uses a **thermometer** to take my temperature.

thin

Tim is very **thin**. He is not fat. This book is **thin**. It has only ten pages.

thorn

Some plants have **thorns**. **Thorns** are sharp.

thread
threaded, threading

Sally can **thread** a needle.
She is using blue **thread**.

thunder

Thunder is a loud noise.
It comes with lightning.

tiger

A **tiger** is a large wild cat.
It has stripes on its body.

through

The dog walks **through** the big pipe.

ticket

I must buy a **ticket** before I get onto the train.

tight

Norman's shirt is too **tight** for him.

throw
threw, throwing

Harry will **throw** the ball to you.

tidy
tidied, tidying

I will **tidy** my room.
I will put everything away.

time

Do you know what **time** it is?
It is one o'clock.

thumb

You have a **thumb** on each hand.

tie
tied, tying

Sandra can **tie** a bow in her hair.
Father wears a **tie** to go to work.

tin

There is milk in this **tin**.
These things are made of **tin**.

tiny

Tiny means very small.  The elephant thinks that the spider is a **tiny** insect.

toast   toasted, toasting

Toast is bread cooked till the outside is hard.
Norman has **toasted** the bread.

toilet

We need to go to the **toilet** many times every day.

tired

Father is **tired** after working all day.
He is trying to sleep.

today

Today is Monday.

tomorrow

Tomorrow is Tuesday.
Tomorrow is the day after today.

to

Sandra runs **to** the slide.
She is going **to** go down the slide.
Her mother is talking **to** her friend.

toe

I have a sore **toe**.

together

Three cats are eating **together**.
One cat is eating by himself.

tongue

You taste food and speak with your **tongue**.

tonight

Tonight is the evening of today.
My mother and father have gone out **tonight**.

tool

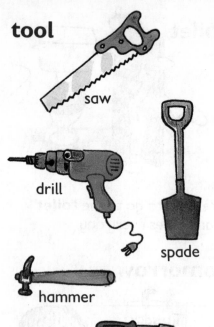

saw

drill

spade

hammer

screwdriver

spanner

compasses

axe

penknife

screw

pliers

nail

A **tool** helps us to work.
These are Uncle Bill's **tools**.

tooth   teeth

The baby has one **tooth** now.
Soon he will have more **teeth**.

toothbrush   toothbrushes

We use a **toothbrush** to clean
our teeth.

top

Polly is at the **top** of the ladder.
Brian is playing with a **top**.

torch   torches

Uncle Bob is carrying a **torch**.
A **torch** is a lighted piece of
wood.

tortoise

A **tortoise** has a hard shell.
It moves very slowly.

touch   touched, touching

Sally **touches** the flower with
her hand.

towel

I dry myself with a **towel** after
my bath.

town

A **town** has many streets and houses.
It also has shops, offices, schools and supermarkets.

toy

Harry has a **toy** to play with.

traffic

There is a lot of **traffic** on the road.

train

The **train** is arriving at the railway station.

trap   trapped, trapping

We want to catch a mouse in this **trap**.
We will **trap** it.

tray

Polly is carrying the glasses on a **tray**.

treasure

They found the **treasure** when they were digging.
What a lot of jewels and money!

tree

A **tree** is a big plant.
Here are some **trees**.

pine

mango

palm

willow

triangle

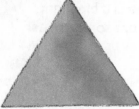

A **triangle** is a shape with three sides.

truck

A **truck** carries heavy loads. This **truck** is full of sand.

try
tried, trying

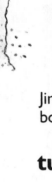

Jimmy will **try** to reach the book.

tricycle

A **tricycle** has three wheels. Sandra is riding a **tricycle**.

true

A **true** story tells about things that really happened.

tube

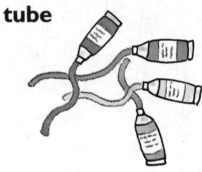

Rita has bought some **tubes** of paint.

trip
tripped, tripping

Tim **tripped** over a stone and fell.

trumpet

Toby is learning to play the **trumpet**.

tulip

A **tulip** is a flower. **Tulips** are grown mainly in Holland.

trousers

His **trousers** are too long.

trunk

The **trunk** is the thickest part of a tree.
The elephant's nose is called a **trunk**.

turkey

A **turkey** is a large bird. **Turkey** is good to eat.

turn
turned, turning

I **turn** the handle to open the door.

untidy

My room looks very **untidy**. I must put everything away.

turtle

A **turtle** has a hard shell. Most **turtles** live in the sea.

ugly

The witch is very **ugly**. I do not like to look at her.

umbrella

An **umbrella** keeps you dry when it is raining.

twinkle
twinkled, twinkling

Can you see the stars **twinkle** at night?

under

Dick is hiding **under** the table.

uncle

Your **uncle** is the brother of your father or mother.

two

Norman is holding **two** buns, one in each of his **two** hands.

unkind

It is **unkind** to pull a dog's tail.

uniform

A policeman wears a **uniform**. A soldier wears a **uniform** too.

up

Harry is walking **up** the hill.

use   used, using

We will **use** a knife to cut the cake.

vase

I will put these flowers in a **vase**.

upside down

Mrs. Lee is reading the book **upside down**.

vegetable

potato

chilli

cabbage

green pepper

sweet potato

cucumber

long beans

onion

peas

upstairs

I can see many things from the window **upstairs**.
We are going **upstairs**.

vacuum cleaner

Mrs. Lee uses a **vacuum cleaner** to clean the carpet.

van

The men brought the cupboard in a **van**.

Which **vegetables** do you like to eat?

106

very

I am wet.
My sister is **very** wet.

violin

Patrick is playing a **violin**.

vet

A **vet** looks after animals when they are sick.

visit
visited, visiting

We **visit** our grandmother every week.
We go to her house.

wait
waited, waiting

Don't go yet.
Please **wait** for me.

village

A **village** is a small town.

voice

I can hear my father's **voice**.
He is calling me.

volcano
volcanoes

Hot rocks, fire and smoke sometimes come out of a **volcano**.

wake   woke, waking

Sandra will **wake** her grandfather.
He must get up.

walk
walked, walking

We **walk** on two feet.
A cat **walks** on four feet.

wall

Toby will hang this picture on the **wall**.

wand

The fairy waved her magic **wand** and the frog changed into a prince.

want   wanted, wanting

We are thirsty.
We **want** a drink.

warm

It is **warm** when the sun shines.

wash   washed, washing

Dick will **wash** his hands with soap.
He needs a **wash**.

washing machine

A **washing machine** washes clothes for us.

waste   wasted, wasting

Do not **waste** water.
Turn off the tap when you have washed your hands.

watch   watched, watching

We are **watching** the puppet show.
I look at my **watch** to see what time it is.

water

Water is for drinking and washing.
Water makes plants grow.
Rain is **water**.

watermelon

A **watermelon** is a large fruit.
It tastes sweet.

wave waved, waving

Patrick **waves** goodbye to his friends.
The **waves** are splashing against the rock.

way

This is the **way** to the zoo.

we us, our

Father and I call the dog.
We call the dog.
The dog comes to **us**.
It is **our** dog.

wear wore, wearing

I like to **wear** dresses.
My brother **wears** shorts.

weak

Tim is **weak**.
He is not strong enough to lift the box.

weather

In some countries the **weather** is hot.
In other countries it is cold.

web

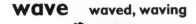

The spider traps insects in its **web**.

weed weeded, weeding

Father will **weed** the garden.
Weeds are plants that grow where we do not want them.

week

There are seven days in one **week**.

weekend

Saturday and Sunday are the **weekend**.

weigh weighed, weighing

Norman is **weighing** himself.

welcome

"**Welcome**," says Sally.
She is glad to see her friend.

whale

A **whale** is a large animal.
Whales live in the sea.

where

Where is Toby?
He is behind the bush.

well

Rita sings **well**.
People like to hear her sing.
You can get water from the **well**.
Betty has done good work.
"**Well** done," says the teacher.

what

"**What** is that?" asks Mrs. Lee.

which

Which dress shall I choose?

wheel

That is Jimmy's bicycle **wheel**.

whisker

A cat has **whiskers** on its face.

wet

Sandra is **wet**.
She fell into the pool.

when

When do you go to sleep?
I go to sleep at 8 o'clock.

whisper
whispered, whispering

Polly **whispers** to Sally.
Nobody else can hear what she says.

whistle
whistled,
whistling

He blows the **whistle** before
the train leaves.
Harry **whistles** to his dog.

white

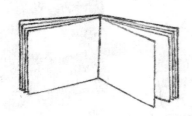

White is a color.
The pages of this book are
white.

who

Who is he?
He is my grandfather.

why

Why is Patrick running?
He is running because he is
late.

wicked

A **wicked** person likes to hurt
people and be bad.

wide

The door is not **wide** enough.
The elephant cannot go
through it.

wild

leopard

deer

rhinoceros

A **wild** animal finds its own
food.
These are **wild** animals.

wild boar

A **wild boar** is a wild pig.
It has small horns by its mouth.

win   won, winning

The first person to finish will
win the race.

wind

The **wind** has blown her hat away.

wire

Wire is made of metal. It can be thin or thick.

woman
women

Your mother is a **woman**. A girl grows up into a **woman**.

window

I must close the **window**. It is raining.

wish   wished, wishing

Toby is making a **wish**. He **wishes** he could fly.

wood

Wood comes from trees. Mr. Smiley is chopping some **wood**.

wing

A bird has two **wings**. An airplane has two **wings** too.

witch   witches

The **witch** in this fairy tale is wicked.

wool

Wool comes from sheep. **Wool** is used for making warm clothes.

wipe   wiped, wiping

Dick **wipes** his wet hands on a towel to dry them.

wolf   wolves

A **wolf** is a wild dog. **Wolves** hunt for food.

work   worked, working

These people **work** in an office. I have a lot of **work** to do.

112

worker

These **workers** are helping to build the house.

world

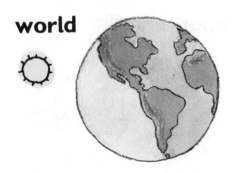

The **world** is another name for the earth.

worm

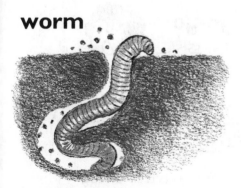

A **worm** is long and soft. It lives in the ground.

worry
worried, worrying

Do not **worry**.
I will help you with the work.

wrap
wrapped, wrapping

Polly **wraps** up the box with blue paper.

wrist

Toby wears a big watch on his **wrist**.

write
wrote, writing

Little Sandra can **write** her name.

wrong

That is the **wrong** piece.
It does not look right.

x-ray

An **x-ray** shows the inside of your body.

xylophone

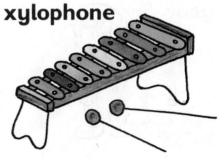

A **xylophone** makes music.
You use a little hammer to play a **xylophone**.

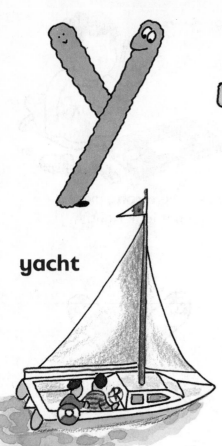

yacht

We go sailing on our **yacht**.

yell   *yelled, yelling*

Uncle Bob is **yelling** at the naughty boys.
Patrick gave a **yell** when he stepped on a nail.

yolk

The **yolk** is the yellow part of an egg.

you   *you, your*

You have a new watch.
Father gave it to **you**.
It is **your** watch.

yawn   *yawned, yawning*

I **yawn** when I am tired.
What a big **yawn**!

yellow

Yellow is a color.
My raincoat is **yellow**.

young

The boy is **young**.
He is only ten years old.
A puppy is a **young** dog.

year

The baby is one **year** old.
There are 365 days in one **year**.

yesterday

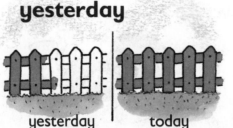

yesterday | today

Yesterday father started to paint the fence.
Today he has finished painting the fence.

yo-yo

A **yo-yo** is a small toy.
It goes up and down on a string.

zoo

You can see many animals at the **zoo**.

zebra

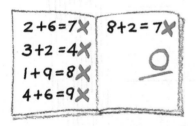

A **zebra** has black and white stripes.

zero

Zero means none at all.

zipper

I pull up my **zipper**.

zoom   zoomed, zooming

The cars **zoom** around the corner.

● The Calendar

DECEMBER
NOVEMBER
OCTOBER
SEPTEMBER
AUGUST
JULY
JUNE
MAY
APRIL
MARCH
FEBRUARY

JANUARY

SUNDAY	MONDAY	TUESDAY	WEDNESDAY	THURSDAY	FRIDAY	SATURDAY
			1	2	3	4
5	6	7	8	9	10	11
12	13	14	15	16	17	18
19	20	21	22	23	24	25
26	27	28	29	30	31	

There are seven days in a **week**.
There are four weeks in a **month**.
There are twelve months in a **year**.

● The Family Tree

This is Harry's family tree.

grandfather　　grandmother

father　　mother　　　　　uncle　　aunt

sister　　Harry　　brother　　　　cousin　　cousin

● Holidays

July 4th
Independence Day　　**Halloween**　　**Thanksgiving Day**　　**Christmas**

● Numbers

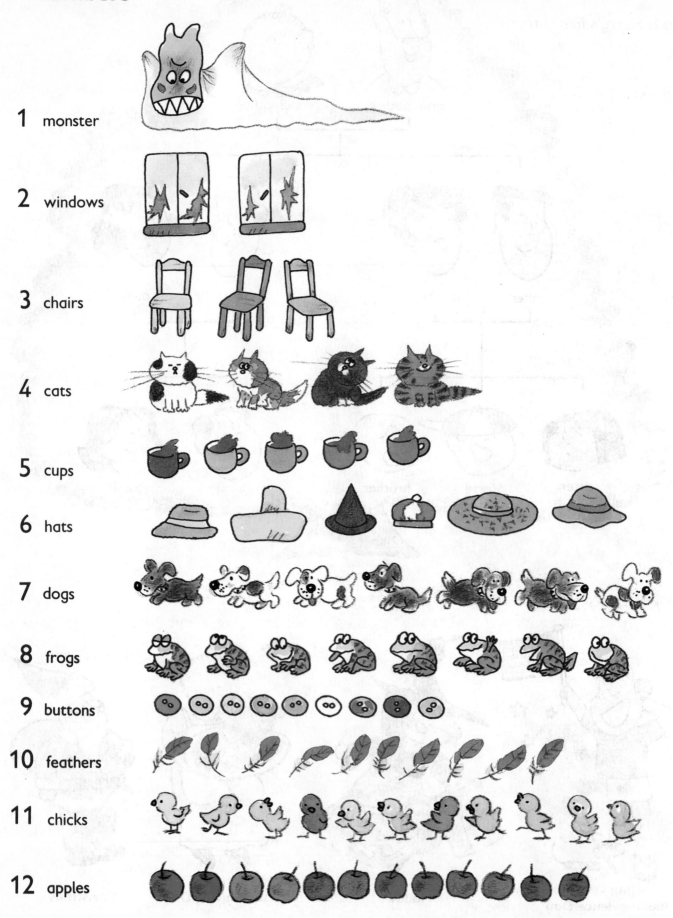

1 monster

2 windows

3 chairs

4 cats

5 cups

6 hats

7 dogs

8 frogs

9 buttons

10 feathers

11 chicks

12 apples

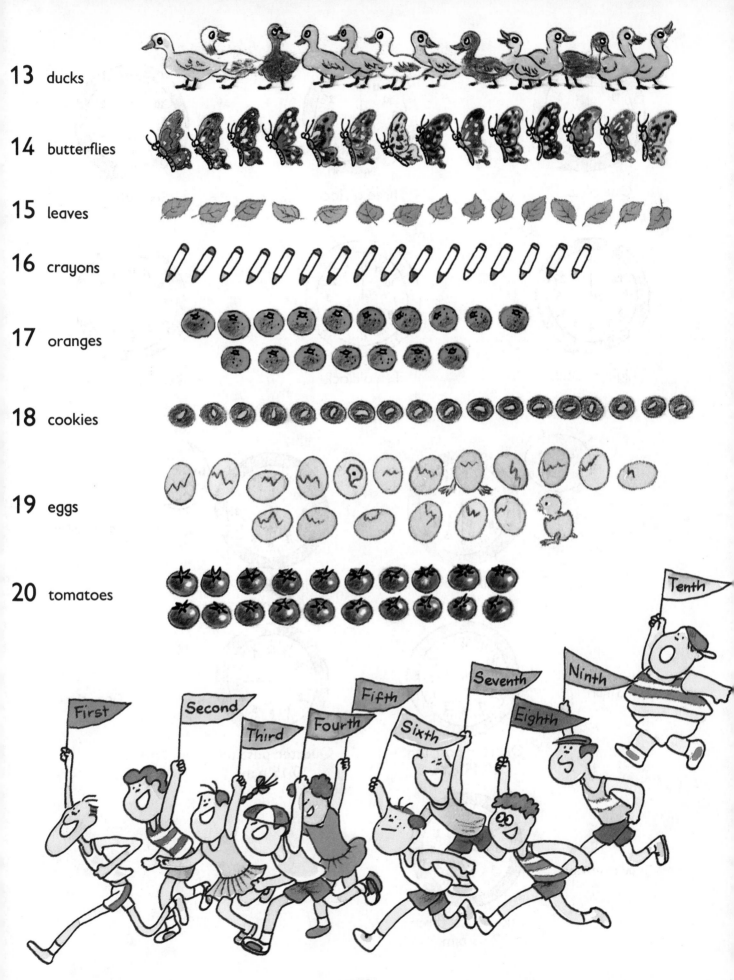

13 ducks

14 butterflies

15 leaves

16 crayons

17 oranges

18 cookies

19 eggs

20 tomatoes

First

Second

Third

Fourth

Fifth

Sixth

Seventh

Eighth

Ninth

Tenth

● Time

One o'clock

Three o'clock

Six o'clock

Eight o'clock

Ten o'clock

Twelve o'clock

Good morning.

Half past six
6.30 a.m.

Good evening.

Half past six
6.30 p.m.

Good morning.

Quarter past ten
10.15 a.m.

Good night.

Quarter past ten
10.15 p.m.

Good afternoon.

Quarter to three
2.45 p.m.

120